SMALL BUT *DEADLY*

DEADLY
BLUE-RINGED OCTOPUSES

By Daisy Allyn

Gareth Stevens
Publishing

WHAT IS AN OCTOPUS?

Octopuses belong to a group of ocean animals called cephalopods (SEH-fuh-luh-pahdz). There are over 250 kinds of octopuses. All octopuses have a large soft head, a soft body, and eight arms. The underside of each arm has two rows of **suction cups**. Octopuses use these to hold on to **prey**.

Octopuses come in many sizes. The smallest—the star-sucker pygmy octopus—is 0.6 inch (1.5 cm) long. The average North Pacific giant octopus weighs about 100 pounds (45 kg)!

DEADLY DATA

The word "cephalopod" is Greek for "head-foot." Other cephalopods include squid and cuttlefish.

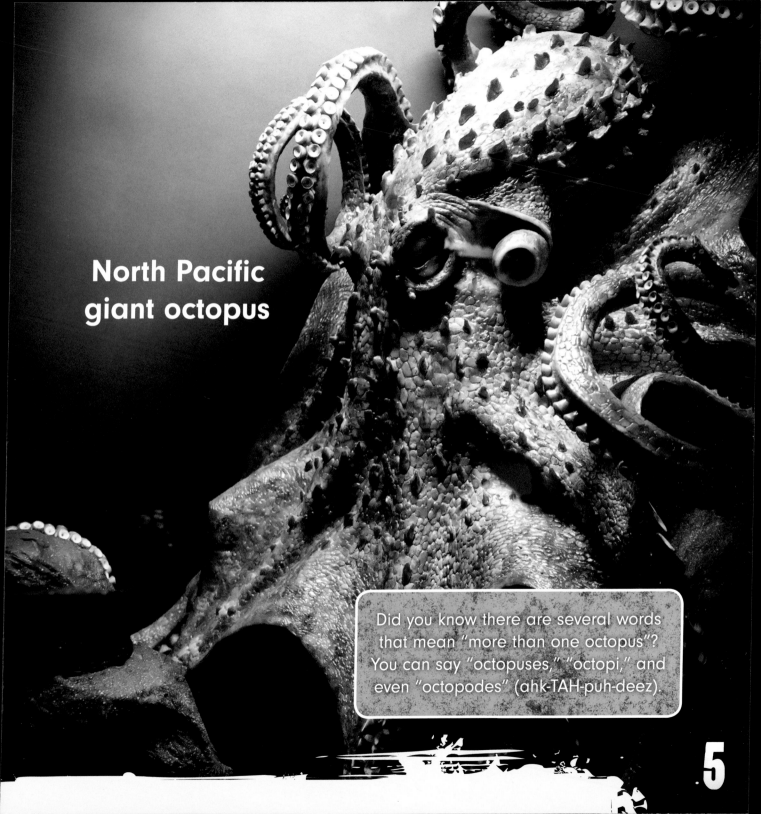

**North Pacific
giant octopus**

Did you know there are several words
that mean "more than one octopus"?
You can say "octopuses," "octopi," and
even "octopodes" (ahk-TAH-puh-deez).

If this tiny octopus wasn't so deadly, you could hold it in the palm of your hand!

THE BLUE-RINGED OCTOPUS

The blue-ringed octopus gets its name from the bright blue rings that appear on its body when it's alarmed. The largest blue-ringed octopus is only about 8 inches (20 cm) from the tip of one arm to the tip of another. Most are about the size of a golf ball.

Blue-ringed octopuses are small and colorful, but they're also highly venomous. They make a liquid called venom inside their bodies. This venom is one of the deadliest in the world.

DEADLY DATA

Like all octopuses, blue-ringed octopuses have no bones. They can fit their soft bodies into some very small places.

7

LESSER AND GREATER

The two most common kinds of blue-ringed octopuses are called the lesser and the greater. The terms "lesser" and "greater" refer to the size of the octopuses' rings, not their bodies. The lesser blue-ringed octopus is larger than the greater blue-ringed octopus, but its rings are smaller.

The lesser blue-ringed octopus is the more common of the two. It lives along the southern coast of Australia. The greater blue-ringed octopus lives in **shallow** water and **tide pools** between northern Australia and southern Japan.

lesser

Blue-ringed octopuses stay close to shore and rarely go out into deep water.

greater

When its rings aren't blue, the blue-ringed octopus blends in with its surroundings.

BLUE RINGS

When the blue-ringed octopus is resting, it has a brown or yellowish-brown color. Its blue rings look like dark patches. Its skin looks bumpy. These features help the blue-ringed octopus hide in cracks and under rocks on the sea bottom.

When a blue-ringed octopus becomes alarmed, the dark patches turn bright blue. The rings look like they're glowing! The blue rings serve as a warning to the octopus's enemies. They say, "Stay away! I'll hurt you!"

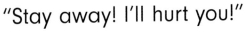

BODY PARTS

The blue-ringed octopus's body is much like the bodies of other octopuses. It has eight arms. Each arm has two rows of suction cups. It has no bones and no shell, so its body is very soft and **flexible**.

The blue-ringed octopus's head and body are covered by baggy skin called the mantle. The skin changes color based on the color of the octopus's surroundings. Inside the mantle are many body parts, including three hearts!

DEADLY DATA

If a blue-ringed octopus loses an arm, it will grow a new one in about 6 weeks!

Greater blue-ringed octopuses, like this one, have a blue line running through each eye.

Blue-ringed octopuses, like most octopuses, come together to make babies just once in their lives.

LIFE CYCLE

Blue-ringed octopuses live for about 2 to 3 years. Once during their lives, male and female octopuses come together to **mate**. The male dies soon after. The female blue-ringed octopus lays between 50 and 100 eggs. She carries them with her and keeps them safe. The babies break out of the eggs in about 50 days. Most baby blue-ringed octopuses are smaller than a pea. The mother octopus dies after the eggs break open because she doesn't eat while keeping the eggs safe.

DEADLY DATA

Baby blue-ringed octopuses are so small they could sit on the head of a match!

DEADLY VENOM

Blue-ringed octopus venom contains toxins—harmful liquids made by living things. The toxins are made by **bacteria** that live inside the octopus's body. The blue-ringed octopus's venom is in its spit.

Blue-ringed octopuses use their venom to kill crabs and other animals they want to eat. They also use their venom to chase away enemies and animals that might want to eat them. One bite from a blue-ringed octopus has enough venom to kill 25 people!

DEADLY DATA

All octopuses are venomous. However, only the venom of the blue-ringed octopus is harmful to people.

Blue-ringed octopuses usually only bite people when they're picked up or stepped on.

Blue-ringed octopus nests are often surrounded by hollowed-out crab and clam shells.

HUNTING AND EATING

The tiny blue-ringed octopus may not seem like much of a hunter, but it's one of the most deadly hunters in the sea. During the day, it hunts small crabs and shrimp. The blue-ringed octopus uses its hard, beak-like mouth to break holes in tough shells. Then the octopus uses its venom to kill its prey and soften the animal's insides. Once the prey is dead, the octopus uses its beak to break the shell and suck up the insides.

DEADLY DATA

Blue-ringed octopuses actually make two kinds of venom. One is specially made to kill crabs—their favorite meal.

PEOPLE AND BLUE-RINGED OCTOPUSES

When blue-ringed octopus venom enters a person's body, it **paralyzes** them. They can't move, and their lungs stop working. The venom also takes away the person's senses of sight and touch. There are no drugs to treat blue-ringed octopus venom.

The effects of a blue-ringed octopus's venom can last up to 24 hours. Someone who has been bitten needs a machine to keep them breathing during that time. Even though they're deadly, some people keep blue-ringed octopuses as pets!

VENOM FACTS

A single blue-ringed octopus bite has enough venom to kill 25 people.

When an octopus bites someone, the person quickly begins to feel sick to their stomach. Soon after that, their sight gets blurry.

The blue-ringed octopus's venom begins working in about 3 minutes.

The blue-ringed octopus's venom can kill a person in less than 30 minutes.

Scientists hope that by studying blue-ringed octopuses, they'll find a drug to treat people who've been bitten by them.

GLOSSARY

bacteria: tiny creatures that can only be seen with a microscope

flexible: easily bent and shaped

mate: to come together to make babies

paralyze: to make something lose the ability to move

prey: an animal hunted by other animals for food

shallow: not deep

suction cup: one of the circular parts on octopuses' arms that grab onto prey

tide pool: a small pool of water left on shore when the ocean tides are low

FOR MORE INFORMATION

BOOKS

Gross, Miriam J. *The Octopus*. New York, NY: PowerKids Press, 2006.

Lunis, Natalie. *Blue-Ringed Octopus: Small but Deadly*. New York, NY: Bearport Publishing, 2010.

WEBSITES

Ocean's Deadliest
animal.discovery.com/convergence/oceans-deadliest/deadliest-creatures/deadliest-creatures.html
Learn about the deadliest creatures in the ocean, including the blue-ringed octopus.

Octopuses
www.globio.org/glossopedia/article.aspx?art_id=65
Read more about octopuses, including the blue-ringed octopus.

INDEX